Here's What People Are Saying about this Book . . .

"In educating investors for over 40 years on the long-term historical trends of financial markets, I have found that those taking advantage of these trends turn out to be the big winners. This book stresses the practical 'how to' approach, using traditional investment vehicles. That's what makes it a winner!"

—**Gerald Gold, Economist**, Financial Lecturer,
Recipient of *New York Times*
Financial Man of the Year Award

"As the Director of one of the leading Continuing Professional Education centers in our state, I highly recommend this unique book. It is practical and easy to read. It is gratifying to know that a great many people will be helped by this book through the accountants and other financial service professionals we serve."

—**Rick Bettencourt**,
Executive Director of Financial Services
Fairleigh Dickinson University

"As an estate planning attorney interested in *wealth transfer*, I am delighted to see the disciplined, organized *wealth creating strategy* employed in this book."

—**Robert A. Bernstein, Esq.**,
Bernstein and D'Arcangelo, P.A.
Host, "30 Legal Minutes," Public Access Cable TV
Former Deputy Attorney General, State of New Jersey

"In helping Corporate America achieve and exceed their goals, I am convinced that having financially secure employees greatly assists in the process. After learning how the 'big picture' of wealth creation can easily be accomplished by the techniques in this book, I enthusiastically recommend it."

—Mark Riesenberg, President
Human Resources Unlimited

"As an accountant to small businesses and individuals for over 25 years, I heartily endorse *The 17 Laws of Successful Investing*. Without these techniques, I have seen people struggle financially. You will refer to this book over and over."

—Robert L. Horn, EA,
Enrolled to practice before the IRS
Past President, NJ Society
of the National Association of Enrolled Agents

"I am extremely grateful for this book as a Certified Financial Planner (CFP). It will help me educate others for years to come. It gets me excited to think of the possibilities people have to improve their lives. This book is practical and gives hope *and* direction."

—Alyce Hackett, CFP

"As consultants to small businesses, we are delighted to see this book. It could help the business owner use their business to create greater personal wealth."

—Bill Schoephoester, District Manager
S.C.O.R.E. (Service Corps of Retired Executives)

"In working with recently outplaced employees, I see an extraordinary need for these individuals to take control of their financial lives. *The 17 Laws of Successful Investing* is a must read in difficult times as well as good times."

—Deborah Arcoleo, Vice President
Outplacement International

"*The 17 Laws of Successful Investing* should be part of everyone's library. I can't think of a better, more useful gift."

—Bernard Geizer, Ph.D., Vice President
Program Evaluation and Management
Research, Inc.

"I consider the book to be excellent—'The Best'."

—Al Hanson, Editor
Al Hanson's Economic Newsletter

"Many books that I have read are written for the author, and yours is written for the reader. It is informative and easy to understand."

—James W. Lammers, Sr. Vice President
National Sales Manager
Security Distributors, Inc.

"*The 17 Laws of Successful Investing* is short, succinct and to the point as Richard Rodman lays out astonishing ways money can be put to work when channeled in the right investment vehicle."

—Reviewer's Bookwatch

The 17 Laws of
Successful Inve$ting

Ignore Them at Your Own Risk

The 17 Laws of Successful Inve$ting

Ignore Them at Your Own Risk

Richard Rodman, CFS, CPC

Alidan Press
215 North Ave. West, Suite 360
Westfield, NJ 07090

Although the author and publisher have made every effort to ensure the accuracy and completeness of information contained in this book, we assume no responsibility for errors, inaccuracies, omissions, or any inconsistency herein. Any slights of people, places, or organizations are unintentional.

All data in this book was compiled from sources believed to be reliable. However, there can be no guarantees of reliability.

All opinions contained herein are opinions of the author and should not necessarily be applied to all individuals. Each individual's situation should dictate its own personalized investment strategy. Investors should check with their financial advisors on all investment, financial and tax matters.

First printing 1996
Second printing 1997

ISBN 0-9651353-2-2
LCCN 96-084039

Typesetting and printing services provided by About Books, Inc., 425 Cedar Street, Buena Vista, CO 81211, (800) 548-1876.

ATTENTION CORPORATIONS, UNIVERSITIES, COLLEGES, AND PROFESSIONAL ORGANIZATIONS: Quantity discounts are available on bulk purchases of this book for training or educational purposes. Special books or book excerpts can also be created to fit specific needs. For information, please contact Alidan Press, 215 North Avenue West, Suite 360, Westfield, NJ 07090, (908) 654-8041.

Dedication

To Linda, Alison and Danielle, who show me every day why my career is just a bonus.

Acknowledgments

I would like to thank Linda Rodman for her input in all phases of this book, from editing to typing to re-editing and re-typing. Her determination in wanting to do this job by herself was inspirational. I would also like to thank Ellen Rosenberg, a renowned author in her own right, for being a good listener and offering ideas and support in the planning of this endeavor. Lastly, I would like to thank Marilyn Ross, of About Books, Inc. in Buena Vista, Colorado, for her assistance in all phases of this project. I knew I was in good hands from the moment we spoke.

Table of Contents

List of Tables

Introduction

If there is one false perception I have witnessed time and again in almost three decades of assisting people financially, it is this—people generally believe that investing and creating wealth are harder and more mysterious than they are. This is the reason for this book. In order to demystify this subject, I recommend working with a compatible investment professional who can add the time, training and temperament needed for success. If you can work effectively as a team, much of the mystery is eliminated once you get to the essence of how certain investments and cash flow systems help you achieve the lifestyle you desire.

It has been my observation that there are three major goals we seek to meet financially in our lifetime:

1. Education of Children
2. Retirement
3. Specific Major Wants or Desires (from weddings to yachts!)

If this book can help solve at least one of the above for at least one person it will have served its purpose. I sincerely hope you enjoy the journey to *and* the destination of financial independence!

LAW 1

To Create Wealth, You Must Have a Plan

In order to accomplish any goal, there must be a plan or strategy. This is especially true in creating wealth, because it is an ongoing process consisting of many continuous, smaller goals. For example, once you have reached a goal to accumulate a specific sum of money, in a specific time frame, the "clock" automatically starts over for the next chosen period of time. At that point, you must have a new plan in place, if

3

appropriate, or a continuation of the previous plan. In other words, we must do as well as we can financially throughout our lives, adjusting our strategy as we go. If you do not consistently move forward, you will *automatically* move backward.

The actual plan or strategy should deal with two types of assets:

1. Assets you have already accumulated up to this time

2. Capital that will come into your hands from income in the future

We will deal with the implementation of the strategy of each of these as we progress in this book. For now, just get organized by thinking about each of these as "buckets" of money.

The first category, assets you have already accumulated, is relatively easy to deal with. You can simply make a list of current assets. This list should include assets in the following categories:

- Checking Accounts
- Money Market Accounts or Funds
- Savings Accounts
- Certificates of Deposit
- Stocks
- Bonds
- Mutual Funds
- Annuities—Fixed and Variable
- Retirement Accounts (IRAs, 401(k)s, etc.)
- Other—Accounts Receivable, Mortgages owned, Partnerships, etc.

These represent the assets you may be able to improve upon in the future. The next category, money that will come to you in the future from your income, is critical to wealth creation. You must be able to transfer money from the income category to the asset category in a disciplined, systematized fashion.

It is at this point that you should know the **Wealth Creation Formula.** It is as follows:

Wealth = The Ability to Save + Good Investments x Time^{SM}

This is the only formula in this book, but it is the most important ingredient in wealth creation. The first portion, "Ability to Save" refers to your income. In your lifetime, your *income* is undoubtedly your biggest asset and it is how you handle that asset which will determine how wealthy you become. What you must do is choose an amount of income monthly that you can invest and then let *nothing* interfere with the process.

Many people I have met have had good intentions in this area, but when push comes to shove, there is always one more thing to buy and thus one more reason not to save or invest. In order for this to work, you must "pay yourself first" each month and then have an automatic system for investing it. How to do this will be discussed later.

The amount should not be too high or too low. You can change it, but keep in mind that you only get out of your "wealth creation system" what you put in. You will be amazed that when you "pay yourself first," you will always be able to pay your necessary expenses each month as long as they are not extraordinarily high or out of line.

The next part of the formula, "Good Investments," is what this book is about and will become more obvious as we go along. Keep in mind for now, that choosing good investments is both an "art" and a "science" and must be monitored for the rest of your life. The good news is that all the tools needed will be found here.

The last item in the formula, "Time," is the trickiest. In short, you should start the process as soon as you can, because time is of the essence. The following example shows why.

This is the story of Frick and Frack, twins who complete college at age 22 and start working. Frick starts immediately to invest $2000 per year and does so for 6 consecutive years and then never invests another dime the rest of his life. His brother Frack does just the opposite. He invests nothing for the first 6 years, but then starts to invest $2000 per year and does so each and every year for the rest of his life. They each have the same rate of return averaging 12% per year. The question I have always posed to people is, "How long does it take Frack's investment account to catch up to Frick's?"

The most common answer is 7 years. The logic is that Frack needs 6 years of input plus one year of interest to catch up to his brother Frick. The correct answer is *33 years!* It is not until they both reach age 60 when Frack's money finally overtakes Frick's. At that point Frick has $765,141 (from a total of $12,000 invested over 6 years) and Frack has accumulated $767,859 (from a total of $66,000 invested over 33 years). The moral of this story is clear. You do as best you can in saving money as early as you can, because *Time* is always of the essence!

Another example of why time is so important in our wealth creation formula is our "penny example." The question I will ask you is the following: "What would you rather have, a check for $10,000 or a check for the total of one penny doubled every day for one 30-day month?" The latter check would be for the total of 1¢, 2¢, 4¢, 8¢, 16¢, 32¢, etc. for 30 days. If you said $10,000 you were wrong, although it would be a nice consolation prize. The penny doubled every day for 30 days would have been the wiser choice. However, when most people see the actual result they cannot believe it until they actually go back and work it out for themselves on a calculator. In a 30-day month, the amount of the check would be $5,368,709! Amazing! In a 31-day month it would obviously total $10,737,418! Talk about being short-changed!

Time does amazing things to money. When asked what was the greatest invention of mankind, Einstein replied "Compound Interest!" A smart fellow, that Einstein.

Time also has great meaning to people reading this book who are at or even over the standard retirement age of 65. Today everyone is living longer and people at this age should still plan on being around for 20 or more years. Americans' number one fear is "outliving their money." Planning on living a longer life than previous generations will help you take a giant step in realizing that time is one of the most important factors in our wealth creation formula.

You need not fear outliving your money if you plan correctly. During working years, picture yourself in an **Accumulation Phase** of life. If done properly, you can then participate in what is called the **Enjoyment Phase.** This example illustrates the point. Assume you invest $900 a month for 20 years and average 12% return per year. You would have $484,200 at that point. Because you had planned well in the Accumulation Phase, you can enter the Enjoyment Phase. In this case, you could now withdraw $4,000 per month or $48,000 per year and after 5 years take out almost $250,000 while watching your principal continue to grow to $548,389! (assuming the same 12%/year growth rate). In 10 years, you have taken out almost $500,000 and your principal is now $661,512. If you live forever you can never outlive your money. It is all in the planning.

Below is listed the value of $10,000 at various rates of return over a 10, 15 and 20-year period. This is a handy chart when projecting results.

Table 1 - Compound Interest
($10,000 Invested)

Year	6%	8%	12%	16%
10	$17,908	$21,589	$31,058	$44,114
15	$23,965	$31,721	$54,735	$92,653
20	$32,071	$46,610	$96,461	$194,600

Below is the value of $1000 invested *each year* for 10, 15 and 20 years at various rates of return.

Table 2 - Compound Interest
($1,000 Invested Per Year)

Year	6%	8%	12%	16%
10	$13,974	$15,645	$19,655	$24,734
15	$24,675	$29,324	$41,754	$59,928
20	$37,936	$49,423	$80,700	$133,846

We have now mentioned all three aspects of the Wealth Creation Formula: Ability to Save, Good Investments and Time. What you need to do in your lifetime is to "Create and Manage Wealth." Generally, at younger ages a person just needs to create wealth (and has lots of time). For this person, the ability to save becomes the most important part of the formula.

For some people, all they need to do is "Manage their Wealth." For these people the ability to employ good investments is key. Their need to save may be significantly less or even nonexistent. The point is that the formula works for one and all no matter where you are financially and without regard to age.

Again:

Wealth = Ability to Save + Good Investments x Time^{SM}

LAW 2

Never Bear Too Much or Too Little Risk

Risk can be defined in many ways. To some, risk is the prospect of losing money. To some at the opposite end of the spectrum, risk is the failure to meet the goal of staying ahead of the ravages of inflation and taxation. To many others risk is somewhere in between.

I have found the healthiest and best attitude toward risk involves the goal of staying ahead of inflation and taxation. Therefore, it becomes best to think of risk more as **fluctuation,** which is the unavoidable price one pays for being in the proper financial markets in order to gain the best real rate of return after inflation and taxation. Assuming one wants the best rate of return, then one must figure out what his or her tolerance level is for fluctuation.

Before implementing any plan or strategy you must know yourself from an investment perspective. This can be described as your "investment personality." In getting a feel for this, I recommend thinking about "sleeping down to your investments." In other words, you should ask yourself how much downside fluctuation could you put up with, percentage-wise, before you get too nervous and can't sleep. Is the answer 10% in any 12 month period, 15%, 20%? This answer will start the process of putting together your final strategy.

I feel it is of utmost importance to think of risk as the failure to meet your overall financial goal. You must at least stay ahead of inflation and taxation. The failure to do so will result in loss of purchasing power and a decrease in your standard of living. Since everyone is living longer, failure to accomplish this could be quite painful indeed. Therefore, you should think in terms of fluctuation (not risk) because you are going to need hedges against inflation and taxation in order to obtain a better standard of living, or even keep the one you have.

Some people think that when you get older fluctuation should be drastically curtailed or even eliminated. This is not true. Again, because we are living longer, there is a greater need to always include hedges against inflation and taxation in your investment portfolio and usually for a lifetime. This creates a continual need for some growth-type vehicles.

To further illustrate this point, if one invests all his money in a non-fluctuating vehicle (bank) at 5%, and inflation is 3% and taxes another 2%, there is zero real rate of return. Wealth building never gets off the ground. Just maintaining wealth can be a problem in this example if interest rates drop or inflation picks up, as the combination of inflation and taxation would exceed return.

Some people have come to me hoping that they will see interest rates rise soon to levels of the early 1980s (double digits) so they can get a high return without fluctuation. However, upon close inspection, we see that interest rates might have been double digits, but we had an inflation rate to match. When adding taxation to the formula, they were actually worse off than when interest came down!

Interest rates may not rise again in that manner in any event. In 1980 the long-term treasury bond hit 8%, and then went a lot higher. Guess what year this long-term rate was 8% prior to this period. The answer happens to be *never*, and that is true all the way back to *1790!* Hopefully by now, you will be ready to define risk in a way that will be beneficial to your wealth creating capabilities.

We can now move forward to measuring fluctuation. I have found that numbering general categories of fluctuation from (1) to (5) will help. A (1) is something where principal does not move, such as a money market account, CD or other fixed-type vehicle. A (2) is generally a fixed income vehicle that does fluctuate, such as a bond. A (3) is the average common stock, a (4) is an item extremely aggressive or potentially aggressive such as commodities, and a (5) is akin to outright speculation or even gambling, using vehicles such as options.

There are, of course, shades of fluctuation in between. For example, a convertible bond might be a 2.5 rather than a 2, or a high dividend-paying stock might be a 2.75 instead of a 3.

You may want to think of fluctuation in terms of the scale below. It will help you focus on one category in relationship to another very easily. The first list labels the 1 to 5 scale. The second list converts the scale to specific generic investment vehicles.

1 - Very conservative (no fluctuation)

2 - Moderate

3 - Growth oriented

4 - Very aggressive

5 - Speculative

The **"Investment Conversion"** list is below. Keep in mind this measurement of fluctuation is approximate and should be used as a general guide.

Money Markets and CDS	1
Short-term Bonds (less than 5 years maturity)	1.5
Intermediate-term Bonds (5-10 years maturity)	1.75
Long-term Bonds (greater than 10 years and dependent upon ratings)	2
Convertible Bonds	2.5
High Dividend-Paying Stocks	2.5-2.75

Growth and Value Stocks	3
Small Cap/Emerging Growth Stocks	3.25-3.5

Note: Add .25 to .50 for foreign investments.

For the purpose of this book we stop here on the 1 to 5 scale, as this is the limit in scope of our recommendation and expertise. For instance, we do not recommend commodities or options. Also notice that investing in gold and/or silver shares is not included. These can be effective hedges for some, although not necessary. If one possesses the desire to include them in the possible universe of investments they would be in the 4 range. Note that we added .25 to .50 for foreign investments. We view foreign investing in a very positive light. The added fluctuation is due to currency fluctuation, smaller markets, etc. It is also important, at this time, to mention that you can invest in all of these investment vehicles through a mutual fund. This makes more sense for most people because of the professional management needed to create the best return. More on this later.

It is *very* important to keep in mind that "you get what you pay for." In other words, from ratings of 1 to 3.5 the long-term return will generally get greater as fluctuation increases. This should be common sense. It is not feasible to achieve a 15% average return with vehicles rated between 1 and 2. We will clarify this when we focus on investment return.

LAW 3

Do Not Fear Investing in the U.S. Economy (Stocks) for the Long Term

Now that we have discussed risk and its ramifications, we can move toward reward. In order to counteract risk of loss of purchasing power and ultimate decline in standard of living, we must come up with the proper vehicles to enhance reward. We will start off with historically one of the best—stocks.

If we use 1954 as a starting point with the dollar worth exactly $1.00 and move time-wise 40 years later to 1994, we will find out that the dollar is worth approximately one-sixth of its 1954 value. Therefore we would have needed something to go up approximately 6 times during those years as an offset to inflation. Did stocks go up 6 times? No. They went up **60** times! That's right, they went up on average ten times more than was needed. That performance will obviously also cover the ravages of taxation and with a lot left over for "real" growth and progress.

Table 3 gives a spectacular long-term view of inflation. *From 1940 to 1990 the dollar turned into a dime!*

Table 3 - Loss of Purchasing Power of $1

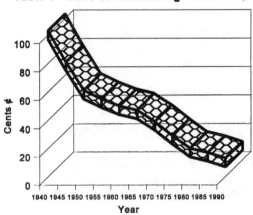

The best example of why not to fear investing in the U.S. economy (stocks) for the long run will now be illustrated. See Table 4. According to Ibbotson Associates, a statistical research firm for the investment industry:

If you invested $1 in 1926 in *inflation*, almost 70 years later it would be $8.35. In other words, inflation during that period went up over 8 times. If you invested $1 in 1926 in Treasury Bills, almost 70 years later it would be worth $12.19. If you invested $1 in 1926 in the average large company stock (Dow Jones-type stocks) you would have $810.54 almost 70 years later! And, if you would have invested $1 in 1926 in the average small company stock, you would have an unbelievable $2,842.77!! Case closed.

Table 4 - Investing $1

Investing $1 in 1926	Value of $1 (1994)
Inflation	$8.35
Treasury Bills	$12.19
Average Large Company Stock	$810.54
Average Small Company Stock	$2842.77

Yes, there were many ups and downs along the way. However, and this is most important, there has *never* been any single event in the history of the United States which has affected any of the investment markets for a long period of time. Even the Great Depression saw stock market averages bottom out slightly over 3 years from the date of the Great Crash. It did take several years after that for them to recover fully, but recover they did. It turned out to be an unprecedented opportunity which may never be duplicated. Capitalism always regenerates itself.

Armed with this knowledge that single events do *not* affect prices long-term, we can with confidence know that downturns are opportunities *not* panic situations. The difference between opportunity and panic is everything. It is the difference between building wealth and destroying it.

Bradlee Perry, a partner in David L. Babson & Co., stated "The only thing we know for sure about the stock market is that it trends strongly upward over the long term. This is completely predictable, while the timing and magnitude of downswings are unpredictable." We might add: And the downswings don't last long and are not tied to single events.

We are now in a position to summarize the **risk vs. reward** scenario using historical data.

The chance of losing money in the average stock investment in any given year is 24%. This is quite logical as the market is usually up 3 out of every 4 years. However, if you hold the average stock for 5 years the odds of losing money drop to 6%! In other words, the odds of making money are 94%. If holding for ten years, the chance of losing money in the average stock drops to 1% and in 20 years the chance of losing is zero! The odds on making money in those time frames are 99% and 100% respectively! See Table 5.

If you now couple the reward side of this example with the risk side, it becomes quite interesting. The chance of earning an excellent return (defined as at least 10% per year on average) is 57% in any one year. In other words, the odds are with you right from year one. They are greater than 50-50 that you will make at least a 10% average annual return. The odds of this excellent annual return rise the longer stocks are held and hit a high probability of almost 80% over 20 years. See Table 6.

Table 5 - Odds of Losing Money

Holding Period	Odds of Losing Money in Average Stock (S&P 500)
1 year	24%
5 years	6%
10 years	1%
20 years	0%

Table 6 - Odds of Earning an Excellent Return

Holding Period	Odds on Earning 10% or More Annually in the Average Stock
1 year	57%
5 years	64%
10 years	70%
20 years	78%

No wonder it pays to invest in America. Hopefully, these examples have greatly reduced any and all lingering fears. All investing is made up of **greed** and **fear.** We need to overcome fear to be successful. At the same time, greed will be controlled as well so that you can expect *reasonable* returns.

LAW 4

Never Invest for Less Than 5 Years

In today's fast-paced world, long-term has for some investors come to mean 4-6 hours. This, of course, is an exaggeration, but the point is that almost all people have a shortened view of investment time frames. When asked what is the optimum time frame to hold an investment, world renowned investor Warren Buffet replied "Forever." This is fundamentally true, but most people cannot relate to this.

I have found that the "happy medium" for investors' forward vision should be 5 years. **You should invest for 5 years at a time.** At the end of 5 years, all that really happens is that another 5-year cycle begins. Unless your goals have changed or performance is poor, there would be no logical reason to change your investments. One 5-year cycle leads to the next, which leads to the next, etc. Before you know it, Warren Buffet's "Forever" holding period becomes a reality and optimum performance is achieved.

We use 5 years because anything less would not coincide with a whole business and financial market cycle, from bull market to bear market and back to bull market. Anything greater than 5 years becomes difficult for the average person to relate to. One must get to the finish line in increments.

You must also be totally committed for 5 years so that it will take the fear out of investing and you will not be made nervous by events. A simple game will illustrate the minimal impact of events on the stock market over the long run and why the 5-year rule is important. Below is a dated listing of headline events as printed in the *Los Angeles Times*. Without peeking (the answer is upside down at the end) try to guess what year they all took place. The prize will be your surprise!

Month/Day	Headline
Jan. 21	Bond Dealers Doubt the Worst is Over
Feb. 20	Jobless Figure Makes Steepest Jump in 4 years
Mar. 14	Stocks Take Worst Dive in 2 Months

May 24	62 Economists Believe Inflation Will Get Worse
July 3	Interest Rate Fears Weigh Down Stocks
Aug. 6	U.S. Faces Mounting Trade Problems
Oct. 25	Fear Grips Investors But Pros Look to the Future

Answer: 1974!

To further illustrate the value of a 5-year holding period, Table 7 shows the results of investing $10,000 for every single 5-year period from 1955 and ending in 1993. This particular example is the result of investing in a specific mutual fund, the Templeton Growth Fund. This is a representative result of worldwide investing. This particular fund is used because of its long history. The example assumes all dividends and capital gains have been reinvested.

Table 7 - Results of Investing $10,000 Every Single 5-Year Period from 1955

Period Covered (Jan. 1 - Dec. 31)	Value of $10,000 at end of period
1955-1959	$14,878
1956-1960	$15,827
1957-1961	$17,893
1958-1962	$18,621
1959-1963	$13,157
1960-1964	$14,838
1961-1965	$15,921
1962-1966	$12,747
1963-1967	$16,762
1964-1968	$21,966
1965-1969	$20,442

1966-1970	$15,658
1967-1971	$20,159
1968-1972	$29,876
1969-1973	$19,534
1970-1974	$14,354
1971-1975	$21,109
1972-1976	$25,406
1973-1977	$18,143
1974-1978	$24,010
1975-1979	$34,634
1976-1980	$31,689
1977-1981	$21,544
1978-1982	$19,831
1979-1983	$22,110
1980-1984	$17,809
1981-1985	$18,078
1982-1986	$21,970
1983-1987	$20,443
1984-1988	$19,011
1985-1989	$22,805
1986-1990	$16,230
1987-1991	$17,582
1988-1992	$17,771
1989-1993	$19,079

Do you see any values totaling less than $10,000 in the last column? No, not even close. In this example you always made money. The worst 5-year period was 1962-1966 as the value was "only" $12,747. In that 5-year period you caught 2 bear markets—1962 and 1966. However, with 3 up years and 2 down years you were still able to come out ahead.

The best 5-year period was 1975-1979 when the value of $10,000 became $34,634. This was due to the fact that the previous bear market lasted a long time (2 years) as it covered 1973 and 1974.

Does it pay to have a 5-year holding period? Only if you want to make money! As we said before: One 5-year period leads to the next and so on. Table 8 shows the same set of circumstances for every 20-year period from 1955.

Table 8 - Results of Investing $10,000 Every 20-year Period from 1955

Period Covered (Jan. 1 - Dec. 31)	Value of $10,000 at end of period
1955-1974	$77,367
1956-1975	$99,472
1957-1976	$139,507
1958-1977	$202,081
1959-1978	$161,891
1960-1979	$180,110
1961-1980	$199,175
1962-1981	$167,978
1963-1982	$215,206
1964-1983	$272,063
1965-1984	$216,180
1966-1985	$226,155
1967-1986	$289,524
1968-1987	$262,466
1969-1988	$235,466
1970-1989	$241,166
1971-1990	$234,427
1972-1991	$252,517
1973-1992	$156,120
1974-1993	$229,982

Not only are there no negative returns but it becomes easier to see why Warren Buffet said the optimum holding period is "Forever." Since everyone is living longer it is not inconceivable that a person retiring today at age 65 will see four 5-year cycles or a total of 20 years. Thus, planning still requires this long-term horizon even for the retired investor.

In looking at returns of various investment categories for every 20-year period from 1932 (i.e.: 1932-1951, 1933-1952, etc.) the following is revealed:

Worst 20-Year Period (Average Annual Return)

Large Stocks	6.8%/year
Small Stocks	8.2%/year
Corporate Bonds	1.3%/year
Treasury Bills	.4%/year

The worst you would have done in any 20-year period investing in the S&P 500 index is to quadruple your money!

Best 20-Year Period (Average Annual Return)

Large Stocks	16.9%/year
Small Stocks	21.1%/year
Corporate Bonds	10.1%/year
Treasury Bills	7.7%/year

Average Annual Return

Large Stocks	12.2%/year
Small Stocks	17.4%/year
Corporate Bonds	5.7%/year
Treasury Bills	3.7%/year

To give you added long-term perspective, if a middle-aged person (age 45) lives to age 85, and the Dow-Jones Average averages 8% per year appreciation, which is historically accurate, that person will see the Dow Jones Average *over 100,000* in his lifetime!

Hopefully, you can now see the reason why if someone comes to us and wants to invest money for a 6 month, 1-year or even 2-year period, we send them elsewhere. We don't know what might happen in the short run, but this "medium run" of 5 years should improve the odds dramatically of realizing an excellent return. Of course, the 5 years will then hopefully stretch to 10, then 15, and 20 and so on.

LAW 5

Only Buy Individual Stocks If You Have Time to Invest in Addition to Money

There is absolutely nothing wrong with buying individual stocks. However, the vast majority of people who do well investing in individual stocks invest a tremendous amount of time in addition to money. We have all heard stories of people who do well investing

31

in individual stocks. However, when compared to proven professionals there are far more people who do poorly and many who literally lose vast sums. We seem to only remember those who do well because their returns are appealing to us, as they appeal to our greed. The risk to attain them is often not considered.

What also catches our eye are low-priced stocks. It *seems* logical that it would be much easier for a $1 stock to go to $2 or a $5 stock to go to $10, so it seems like we should try it. In fact, just the opposite is true. $50 stocks more easily go to $100 than $5 stocks go to $10.

No matter what niche of stock investing you would like to try, it takes time, training and temperament and should only be pursued by people who are totally dedicated. Even then there is no guarantee that you will do anywhere near as well as even the average money manager.

This is due to one fact that almost everyone over-looks. It is a lot easier to buy a stock than it is to *sell* a stock. Anyone over age 18 can call a stockbroker, open an account and instruct the broker to buy any stock traded in the U.S. The money is *not* made on the buy side. **Money is made on the sell side only.** The problem is, amateurs generally don't have any kind of sell strategy. Even if they do, it is usually arbitrary and subjective ("I'll sell when I make 10%") and not tied to analysis of the company's prospects.

This brings us to the next point. Amateurs do not usually bring to the table or even understand the discounting concept. This concept means that the marketplace discounts 6 to even 12 months in advance about the prospects of a company. In other words, the company and the stock are often not in "synch" with each other. People tend to forget that they are buying the stock and not the company. This takes a special type of analysis. Hopefully you can now begin to see why the whole process of investing in individual stocks is so hard.

There is an old expression "Never confuse brains with a bull market." When stocks in general are rising it is much easier to think you can accomplish successful individual stock investing. However, the true measure of how one will do in the long run is dependent on how one performs when markets are going against them. Do they have the emotional and intestinal fortitude to believe in a certain system or method of individual stock investing that will hold them in good stead during unsteady times? Probably not, especially when compared to a proven professional.

The key element in all this is risk management. As an interesting example we can examine the following. Let's suppose one completes 20 transactions in individual stock investing. We will also assume that the results are such that you have 10 winners and 10 losers *in any order*. We can further assume that the winners are all 10% and the losers also lose 10% each. If you start off with $1,000, how much money do you have left after these 20 transactions?

If you guessed $1,000 you are almost correct. The answer is $904. Now, however, we will assume the same basic scenario, except that all the gains are 40% and each of the losses are also 40%. If you guessed that you have about the same result figuring everything is still balanced, you are way off. The correct answer is $175! That's right. You are almost wiped out! It doesn't seem that this answer could possibly be correct, but it is.

During many market cycles you will be right only 50% of the time, if that. The question is, have you mastered a strategy of managing risk that will get you through it profitably? Is investing in individual stocks starting to sound more difficult?

An additional example can amplify the importance of this law. If a $10 stock drops to $5, you have lost 50%. However, in order for it to recover to $10 it has to go up 100%. Historically, this is infinitely harder to do and unless you have the expertise and have put in the time to develop a sound risk management strategy, you easily can be caught in the cycle of a number of small winners with some large losses. "Some large losses" is all you need to never be able to get back in the game.

LAW 6

Mutual Funds—The Vehicle of Choice for Most People

Experience shows that for most people mutual funds make the most sense. Even if choosing mutual funds, however, one must still invest time in the process. It does not take as much time as investing in individual stocks, but efficient, quality time is still needed. After all, there are over 7,500 mutual funds with new funds opening daily.

In fact, the process is complex enough that for most investors, I recommend working with an investment professional who specializes in mutual funds and who can assist in assembling portfolios for maximum long-term benefit. It would result in poor performance to simply read the latest investment magazine listing the #1 performer for the past year and invest in it for the coming year. History has shown that the #1 performer last year has a great probability of becoming a poor performer shortly. There is more that goes into the process which will be discussed later.

The purpose of this law is to convince you that mutual funds should be your vehicle of choice either for all your liquid capital or at least most of it. A list of ten reasons is below. For those of you already owning mutual funds this will be a good review of the benefits.

1. Professional Management
2. Diversification
3. Liquidity
4. Low Cost (in any type of fund)
5. Easy Entry
6. Automatic Investment Plan
7. Automatic Reinvestment of Dividends and Capital Gains
8. Systematic Withdrawal and Automatic Exchange Plans
9. Simple Record Keeping
10. No Insolvency

Professional Management

You are hiring a complete and total professional to manage your money. If you pick the right professionals, you will undoubtedly, over time, do very well. If you find that you made a mistake and did not pick the right money managers, you can fire them and hire others. It's that simple. You are counting on the fund manager(s) to perform in a manner consistent with the objective of a particular fund or funds, by buying and selling the underlying securities (stocks, bonds, etc.) that they have been entrusted with.

Diversification

Diversification will be thoroughly discussed in Law 8. In a mutual fund this is a very key benefit. By owning parts of well-managed businesses you can greatly reduce the risk of investing in any one business that could have a serious or permanent downturn. Some mutual funds own hundreds of positions in many industries with varying themes relating to size, geography, etc.

Liquidity

Hopefully you will be following Law 4 and investing for a minimum of 5 years. However, even if you are, there could conceivably come a time when you need money ahead of schedule. With mutual funds you have your choice: either write for it or call for it. Either way, your liquidity needs are met in very short order (several business days). If you wish to call for it, you must check off the proper box on the application. I recommend actually writing for it and not having the capability to call so you do not have the temptation to move money when it would not be in your best interest.

Low Cost (In Any Type of Fund)

The type of mutual fund bought (load, no load, low load, no initial load, etc.) doesn't really matter. They are all low-cost if you are happy with the net result! It is amazing to me that we can all participate in these wonderful vehicles and hire the best money managers in the world to manage our money at such a low cost, one low enough to give us great *net* returns, which is all that really counts.

The important thing to decide is whether you can spend the *time*, obtain the necessary *training*, and acquire the *temperament* needed (the 3 T's) to do the job yourself. This is unlikely and even undesirable for most people. You most likely need to work with a professional you feel comfortable with, one who will be worth it many, many times over no matter what structure fund you choose. When there is no one around to guide you through the inevitable rough times you might wind up selling in a panic at exactly the wrong time. It is obviously *not cost* you are concerned with, but *value* in how you go about investing your money. Many people confuse price with value in plotting their financial future, and it can be extremely wealth-inhibiting.

Easy Entry

Minimums in mutual funds are quite low, many in the hundreds of dollars, and you needn't worry about odd amounts. They will calculate how many shares can be purchased for any amount.

Automatic Investment Plan

This is the key to wealth accumulation. "Out of sight, out of mind" investing is best, whereby you can direct the fund to withdraw a set amount from your checking account and deposit it in the fund of your choice each month or quarter automatically. This can also be done manually but I would only recommend that for additional lump sums.

Automatic Reinvestment
of Dividends and Capital Gains

Dividends are the pass-through of stock dividends and bond interest to you the shareholder. Capital gains are gains from the sale of the underlying securities for a profit. Both dividends and capital gains are reinvested automatically to give you the advantage of compounding and leverage, both keys to wealth accumulation. Keep in mind that when dividends and capital gains are declared, your price per share, or net asset value, will decline by the amount of the distribution.

Systematic Withdrawal
and Automatic Exchange Plans

When it comes time to live off your investments, each fund has a systematic withdrawal plan whereby you can designate the amount needed monthly, and they will send a check to you, or in many cases, directly into your checking account. Be sure when implementing this benefit not to request too much money, as the excess will accumulate in lower return vehicles such as savings, checking or money market. The feature of the Automatic Exchange can be used in situations where you desire money to be moved periodically and automatically from one fund in a "family" to another.

Simple Record Keeping

Depending on the fund you are in, you will receive statements monthly, quarterly, or annually. In addition, you will receive statements when you deposit money or withdraw money. You will also receive statements when dividends or capital gains are declared.

Statements issued more frequently than annually are cumulative and all statements are easy to understand. Some have the actual value of the account, while some have the number of shares and price per share. If the latter is the case, you need to have these two numbers multiplied to get the value. You do not need to follow your funds every day in the newspaper. Quarterly is more than enough. Since we're investing for years at a time, following them daily, weekly, etc. is a waste of valuable time. In fact, if you do that, you will be more inclined to make changes when you should not. You would be better off and get more enjoyment out of reading the sports pages, cartoons, or entertainment section on a daily basis!

No Insolvency

An often overlooked benefit of mutual funds is that a mutual fund itself cannot become insolvent. An underlying security, of course, could go up or down, even to extremes, but the management company's fortunes as a business do not affect the value of your shares.

LAW 7

Reduce Taxes Where You Can: But Never Make an Investment Decision Based Solely on Taxes

In the 1970s and 1980s it seemed some investors would invest in anything as long as it had a tax write-off. Sometimes it even had a tax write-off in excess of the investment. We are glad those days are over as there was very little economic viability in many of those types of investments.

Taxes are a concern, but they should never be the overriding factor. Let us examine how, with two mainstream-type investment vehicles, we can limit our tax liability and add those dollars to our bottom line.

For the first one, let's calculate exactly how much can potentially be saved by *deferring* taxes. We will assume that we invested $10,000 for 20 years at an average annual return of 12% in a growth-type mutual fund. We will also assume we are in a 33% combined tax bracket (Federal and State).

In this example, we will further assume that taxes were paid on profits *each year* (dividends and capital gains) as is ordinarily the case. At the end of 20 years the $10,000 investment under these assumptions is worth $46,610. Not bad. $10,000 with a 3% per year inflation rate is only $13,439. Therefore, the real dollar return of $33,171, is over 3 times the initial investment.

Next, let's assume the same set of circumstances with one change. Instead of paying taxes each year, we will pay taxes at the **end** of 20 years. We will still pay taxes at the same rate but pay them when we want to, not when the government wants us to. In this instance, instead of $46,610, we would have $67,929 even *after* paying taxes! This is a result of compounding without the government's interference for all 20 years.

We will now go to the ultimate level and assume that we do not pay taxes each year or at the end of 20 years, but that we *continue to defer* taxes. Using this method we would actually have a "pot" of $96,461 to draw down from during our retirement! (See Table 9)

Table 9 - Deferring Taxes (Example 1)

Assumptions

Investment:	$10,000 at 12% per year avg. annual return
Time:	20 years
Tax Bracket:	33%

Results

Pay Tax Each Year:	$46,610
Pay Tax in 20 Years:	$67,929
Defer Taxes:	$96,461

If you were lucky enough to find a truly spectacular growth-type vehicle that was able to average 15% per year, Table 10 will show you an even more amazing result.

Table 10 - Deferring Taxes (Example 2)

Assumptions

Investment:	$10,000 at 15% per year avg. annual return
Time:	20 years
Tax Bracket:	33%

Results

Pay Taxes Each Year:	$67,929
Pay Taxes in 20 Years:	$112,956
Defer Taxes:	$163,665

In this last example the difference between paying taxes each year and deferring taxes is almost $100,000! This is on a relatively small investment of $10,000. Can you imagine if this were $100,000 that was invested. The difference between paying taxes when you want rather than when the government wants is almost $1,000,000!!

Here is another way of looking at the same tax issue. We assume that there are two brothers, Frick and Frack (sound familiar?). Each brother has a lump sum of $50,000 and the contest between them is to see who can total $500,000 faster. Frick invests in something that yields him an average 12% per year return and he does *not* pay taxes. His brother, Frack, invests in the same vehicle but has to pay taxes each year in a 33% total tax bracket. In this example it takes "No-taxes Frick" approximately 20 years to get from $50,000 to $500,000. However, it takes Frack about 30 years to get to the same amount. In other words, due to paying taxes each year, it took him an entire extra decade! Talk about wasted time.

You might now be asking, "What is this tax-deferred account?"

Some of the top money managers in the world will accept and manage your money in a separate account, separate from their regular mutual fund. In this account, you do *not* have to pay any taxes on dividends and capital gains, as long as the money is left in.

This vehicle is called a Tax-Deferred Variable Annuity. Simply put, it is a mutual fund where you have an option to turn it into an annuity in order to receive monthly income for life. I do not recommend exercising this option, but merely using this vehicle as a mutual fund and taking money out of it when needed. This way you do not commit to an inflexible program of receiving payments of principal and interest for life, which may be more or less than your needs at the time. If payments are more than your needs, you wind up paying taxes on the earnings of money not spent. If the payments are less than your needs, your standard of living suffers.

The government has placed one major restriction on withdrawing funds in these accounts. If you take money out before age 59½, which is the same age as other retirement plans, you will be hit with a 10% IRS penalty. For this reason you should only invest money in these accounts that is longer term money to avoid the government penalty and take advantage of tax-deferral. In addition, the companies issuing these vehicles will impose a penalty for taking out too much money too soon, usually in the first 7 to 8 years, which is another reason to consider these investments long-term.

These accounts are joint ventures between investment firms and insurance companies in order to manage your money and offer the annuity respectively. Because of the insurance company's involvement, there are other side benefits to you or your family. One such benefit is that these accounts avoid probate, though not estate taxes, at time of death, as they are paid to a named beneficiary immediately.

The second mainstream-type vehicle to affect taxes favorably, I call "tax-free bonds with a dividend rollover plan." Everyone in the world it seems has heard of tax-free bonds. In addition, virtually everyone has heard of tax-free bond funds. Both are excellent vehicles and are wealth creators because taxes that are not paid from their interest or dividend payments can go directly to your bottom line. Instead of having a taxable vehicle at 5% and paying one-third of that in taxes, you get to keep the whole thing. On a $100,000 investment, this totals about $1700/year more in your pocket, each and every year. If you are living off this investment, it obviously can be critical to your ability to pay your bills.

However, if you do not need the money you can go one step further and "leverage" this very conservative vehicle to earn more than the 5%. The more time you have the better this concept works. To illustrate, we will assume you have 20 years. We will also assume a $100,000 investment to showcase the impact of this clever maneuver. First, you must invest the money in a tax-free bond fund. It can be done by investing in individual bonds, but the plan does not work as easily from an administrative point of view. It works best with a mutual fund.

Once you're investing in a tax-free bond fund, the rest is easy. You direct the company to then automatically each month "roll the dividend over" into the same fund family's best and most aggressive growth fund, rather than reinvesting the dividends in shares of the bond fund itself as most people do. What is the impact of doing this? It's nothing short of incredible. Let us examine the results in Table 11.

Table 11 - Tax-Free Bond Fund with Dividend Rollover Plan

Assumptions

Investment: $100,000

Yield: 5%

Time: 20 years

Results with dividends reinvested in additional shares: $265,000!

Results with "dividends rolled over" into growth fund averaging 12% per year *after* paying taxes on the growth portion: $397,270!!

Results with "dividends rolled over" into growth fund averaging 16% per year *after* paying taxes on the growth portion: $569,974!!! (Notice the increase in exclamation points!)

That's right, just by being smarter with the "house's money" you have dramatically increased the return of this conservative vehicle without risking the principal. It is like someone giving you a gift of between $132,270 and $304,974 without doing a thing or increasing risk of principal.

If you want to go one step further, you can take the dividend each month and invest it in a growth vehicle that is tax-deferred. In this case, at the end of 20 years you would have accumulated between $503,492 for the 12% example and $769,191 in the 16% example! Not a bad payoff for just a little creativity!

In summary, there are two ways an investor can gain tax advantage using mainstream- type of investments. One is by using "Mutual Funds Without Taxes," more formally known as Tax Deferred Variable Annuities. These will allow you to pay taxes at a later time in your life, enabling you to accumulate much more capital. This is due to compounding of interest in the intervening years without Uncle Sam's interference. The second is by using a regular tax-free bond fund but with "dividends rolled over" monthly and automatically in a growth fund of the same family.

LAW 8

Never Ever Put All Your Eggs in One Basket

This law is, of course, common sense. As investors we constantly have to struggle with "fear" and "greed," the two emotions which guide our monetary decisions throughout our lives. The balance that is created between these two extremes will dictate how successful we can be.

Diversification of investments will help us keep greed in check and enable us to move on through fear. The following example should help us keep our perspective in this balancing act.

We will assume a person has $10,000 and is able to invest that money at an 8% per year return. In this case, he would have $46,610 in 20 years. The question to be answered is this: "Is that result better (a straight 8% per year return) or would it be better to diversify the $10,000 so that $2,000 is invested in 5 different investments with the following results:

$2,000 is totally lost

$2,000 earns 0% interest

$2,000 earns 8% interest per year

$2,000 earns 12% interest per year

$2,000 earns 16% interest per year

Many people say that logic dictates that it would be the 8% per year example. The correct answer is scenario number two. Even those who guessed correctly, however, are completely surprised at the difference monetarily between the two choices.

Whereas the 8% per year example totals $46,610, the "diversified" model totals an astounding $69,532! The difference alone is almost 2½ times the original deposit. If one invested $100,000 instead of $10,000, the difference in the two results is a small fortune, almost $250,000!

Even after I show this example to people and they see the results, they still can't believe it, so we need to go back over it. The original amounts of the diversified model and their totals are as follows:

Investment	Result
$2,000	$0 (Lost Totally)
$2,000	$2,000 (0% interest)
$2,000	$9,320 (8% interest)
$2,000	$19,292 (12% interest)
$2,000	$38,920 (16% interest)
Total	**$69,532**

Hopefully now you can see why diversification is so important. The returns of 12% and 16% way more than made up for the loss of the first $2,000 and the terrible performance of the second $2,000 (0% return). This is an excellent lesson. *You don't need to be right all the time.*

What you should look to do over the long-term is to have your money grow like a staircase, constantly moving upward. The *only* way I know how to do this, is to put together a **properly diversified portfolio** of investments so that when something invariably hits a bump in the road, there exists a good possibility that something else may be going up to offset it. In that instance you can still get the overall staircase effect. Granted, sometimes the steps can get a little rickety, but hopefully you can see the intent and the long-term effect.

Some people, instead of a staircase, have their money in the shape of a floor, that is, a flat line. This would equate with having all your money in the bank. If your return is 5% and inflation is 3% and taxes are 2%, you can see how the money never really gets off the ground, hence a floor rather than a staircase.

Inflation and taxation are the two "monsters" constantly eating away at returns. You must look to achieve a *real* rate of return above and beyond inflation and taxation. Sometimes the floor turns into a down-sloping handicapped ramp as inflation might escalate to 4% or more, thereby resulting in inflation and taxation being greater than the bank rate of 5% (See Law 2).

Also, as previously mentioned, some people long for the "good old days" in the late '70s or early '80s when interest rates in CDs were 15%. However, with inflation at over 10% and taxes at 7-8%, this was a real wealth-inhibiting environment.

Some people, when we meet them, have their portfolios resembling an EKG. Everyone knows what an EKG looks like, with sharp ups and downs and with little or no eventual upward movement. This would describe a portfolio where different things were done for different reasons, at different times, through different advisors, resulting in poor investment selection and poor diversification. Whether your savings and investments resemble a floor, or an EKG or a combination of the two, the idea is to get to the staircase.

How do you properly diversify to get this desired result? It is obviously worth it to try to find complimentary investments in the right mix *for you* to get the job done. This is done through proper **asset allocation** and **diversification** in generic categories such as the ones previously mentioned in the chapter on risk (Law 2). This includes everything from U.S. Stocks to U.S. Bonds to Foreign Stocks and Foreign Bonds and all the subsets within these general categories. The subsets include growth stocks, high dividend paying stocks, value stocks, government bonds, corporate bonds, long-term bonds, short-term bonds, etc. As discussed, the structure of using mutual funds to participate in these vehicles and accomplish these goals is much preferred.

Is it worth it to try to find the best balanced asset allocation for you? You bet. In a study entitled "Determinants of Portfolio Performance" by Ibbotson Associates, it was discovered that how your portfolio achieves its results is determined by Asset Allocation Policy a whopping 91.5% of the time! Security selection comes in second as a determining factor 5.6% of the time, while market timing is a determining factor only 1.8% of the time. Other reasons account for the small remainder. Even though security selection is only a determining factor 5.6% of the time, it is still a very important determinant of portfolio performance.

For now, it is important to know the "whys" of not putting "all your eggs in one basket." How to allocate assets and diversify your portfolio to achieve maximum results will be examined shortly.

LAW 9

Never Try to Time the Market

It certainly is tempting! Can you imagine if you were able to buy anywhere near market lows and sell anywhere near market highs, getting out of harm's way during corrections and bear markets? Wow! Utopia! Even if you did it half the time, your returns would be astronomical. They would be many more times the normal buy and hold strategy. There is one problem with this. *It absolutely doesn't work.*

After years of interviewing people who have tried, I am convinced of it. Yes, some people have had success for several market cycles in a row, but eventually they get "whipsawed" (buying near market highs and selling near market lows). Simply because no one can predict markets continually. In addition, once whipsawed one tends to get whipsawed two or more times in a row, eating up capital at rapid rates.

Do not confuse market timing with asset allocation. Market timing is jumping in and out of markets, 100% either way. Asset allocation is a long-term strategy of investing monies in various generic categories.

In order to illustrate why market timing does not work, let us examine some real-life situations. The first one involves actual performance results of a specific mutual fund over 20 years. The premise assumes a $5,000 per year investment on both the high day for stocks during that year and also investing the same amount each year on the low day for stocks. The results are telling. (see Table 12)

Table 12 - Investing Each Year
at the Stock Market HIGH

The Worst Case

Date of Market	Cumulative Investment	Value on 12/31
1/11/73	$5,000	$4,226
3/13/74	$10,000	$7,530
7/15/75	$15,000	$14,994
9/21/76	$20,000	$27,275
1/3/77	$25,000	$38,480
9/8/78	$30,000	$50,165
10/5/79	$35,000	$68,272
11/20/80	$40,000	$90,568
4/27/81	$45,000	$94,831
12/27/82	$50,000	$109,932
11/29/83	$55,000	$150,920
1/6/84	$60,000	$159,026
12/16/85	$65,000	$208,083
12/2/86	$70,000	$257,152
8/25/87	$75,000	$268,908
10/21/88	$80,000	$337,173
10/9/89	$85,000	$418,066
7/16/90	$90,000	$384,333
12/31/91	$95,000	$509,643
6/1/92	$100,000	$535,858

Investing Each Year At the Stock Market LOW

The Best Case

Date of Market	Cumulative Investment	Value on 12/31
12/3/73	$5,000	$4,616
12/6/74	$10,000	$8,859
1/2/75	$15,000	$18,624
1/2/76	$20,000	$34,175
11/2/77	$25,000	$46,303
2/28/78	$30,000	$60,937
11/7/79	$35,000	$82,610
4/21/80	$40,000	$110,552
9/25/81	$45,000	$115,542
8/12/82	$50,000	$134,548
1/3/83	$55,000	$185,280
7/24/84	$60,000	$194,749
1/4/85	$65,000	$255,125
1/22/86	$70,000	$315,230
10/19/87	$75,000	$330,057
1/20/88	$80,000	$413,896
1/3/89	$85,000	$513,265
10/11/90	$90,000	$471,908
1/9/91	$95,000	$626,345
10/9/92	$100,000	$657,752

After viewing Table 12, hopefully you have come to the right conclusion. No one could buy, at these two wild extremes (the lowest low or the highest high) each year, and even if they could, would it have been worth it? No, of course not. The average annual difference between these two extremes is only 1.4% per year, and the actual dollar amount is negligible considering the amount invested and the long time frame.

Need more convincing? The second example is even more extraordinary. It was researched by Ibbotson Associates over a 65-year period from 1926 to 1990. Table 13 tells the story.

Table 13 - "Buy and Hold" vs. Timing (1926-1990)

Value of $1 Invested from 1926-1990

Average Common Stock	$727.38
Treasury Bills	$11.40
Average Common Stock *minus the 30 best months*	$11.16

In other words, over a 65-year period, if you tried to time the markets and had missed being in common stocks for 30 specific months (less than 1 month every two years) your result would have been less than if you just put the money in Treasury Bills. You would have wasted 65 years! To bring this concept closer to current times, following are the results in the same scenario from 1980-1990.

Table 14 - "Buy and Hold" vs. Timing
(1980-1990)

Value of $1 Invested from 1980-1990

Average Common Stock	$6.85
Treasury Bills	$2.76
Average Common Stock *minus the 10 best months*	$2.70

In other words, in this recent example, if you missed 10 specific months in 10 years, your result was still less than putting your money into Treasury Bills.

Conclusion: Save your money. Do not try to time the markets. To save even more money, drop your newsletter subscription that "predicts" the market. You need your investments to be working for you around the clock, each and every day. Some days will be bad, but you never know when the good days will take place and you must be invested *before* that happens to be able to take advantage. *It's time in the markets not timing the markets that counts!*

LAW 10

Invest Any Lump Sums Immediately and Use Income to Dollar Cost Average

People often ask *"When should I invest?"* The best answer (now that you've seen the cartoon!) is *"Whenever you have the money."* Since we don't know what tomorrow brings except to know that history has shown we should do well in the long run, then we must be in the markets now, *before* they rise.

Some people say, "Shouldn't I invest money gradually?" This would be a second-best idea. Since markets go up approximately 75% of the time and down 25% of the time, the odds are with you that investing your whole lump sum now all at once will work better. Timing does not matter. An analysis by Cincinnati investment advisor James Gore indicates that keeping most of the money in a low-yielding account while feeding money into an investment slowly can shave your annual returns by 2.2 percentage points compared with investing a lump sum all at once.

In August of 1982 when the Dow Jones Average was below 800, you could have safely made the prediction that, "The Dow will go to 1000. I just don't know when!" If you made this prediction you also could have been ridiculed by the pundits and prognosticators who make a living from *trying* to time markets.

After the Dow hit 1000 (the same year!) you could have safely predicted that, "The Dow will go to 2000. I just don't know when!" For this prediction you would have been much more ridiculed, but you would have been correct. The point is that you would have had to be fully invested to fully take advantage of the movement from 1000 to 2000 on the Dow. You should never be worried about the next 100 points on the downside, but should worry about where your money will be for the next 1000 points on the upside.

Of course, once the Dow hit 2000, you could have safely predicted, "The Dow will be 3000. I just don't know when!" and be ridiculed beyond your wildest imagination. Hopefully, by now you get the idea. By the way, a 1000 point move is not as big as it used to be, as it is a smaller percentage. It is interesting that a 100 point daily move downward (2%) will be the lead story on the news. Isn't it curious that the 1000 point rise that preceded it, gets much less attention?

After your lump sum is invested, you must have a plan for future wealth creation and *let nothing stand in your way*. You must "pay yourself first" *each* month. You must come up with a savings amount which hopefully can be adjusted upward *each* year. It should not and need not interfere with paying your bills. Many people have told me that they picked an amount that they thought might be slightly high, but found it amazing how everything just fell into place and all their bills got paid on time. Money leaks out of everyone's budget, but if you harness it up front, it gets captured and goes to work for you in a dramatic fashion over time.

The process of investing a fixed amount in a fixed time frame (usually monthly) is called **Dollar Cost Averaging**. It is one of the keys to wealth creation. It can be done automatically from your checking account, which is important. It should *not* be done manually as you are bound to miss some months, which will cost you dearly in the end.

Dollar Cost Averaging will automatically purchase shares at high points and low points and many points in between, and will thus flatten out the peaks and valleys and let the long-term upward trend work for you. I would *not* Dollar Cost Average into individual stocks because you never know in which stock you might be "averaging down the drain," into a company that ultimately never recovers. That is not the case with a mutual fund as the whole country would have to collapse to have that kind of catastrophe.

Most people have heard of dollar cost averaging and most know its basics. However, many people could understand it better mathematically and know why it works. We will take a look at a scenario whereby someone invests $1000 per month. The fund starts at $10 per share, declines by 25% to $7.50 per share, and then recovers to the starting point.

Table 15 - Dollar Cost Averaging

Month	Investment	Price	Number of Shares Bought
1	$1000	$10.00	100
2	$1000	$9.50	105
3	$1000	$9.00	111
4	$1000	$8.50	118
5	$1000	$8.00	125
6	$1000	$7.50	133
7	$1000	$7.50	133
8	$1000	$8.00	125
9	$1000	$8.50	118
10	$1000	$9.00	111
11	$1000	$9.50	105
12	$1000	$10.00	100
Total	**$12,000**		**1384**

Total Invested: $12,000
Value of account: $13,840
Profit: $1,840

Magic! The only thing we know for sure about equity markets is that they fluctuate. In addition, throughout history, after falling from any high level, they have always returned to that previous point. Although there is no guarantee for the future, this occurrence has turned dollar cost averaging into the magic wealth creator that it is.

LAW 11

Find Your Correct Asset Allocation Strategy and Review it Periodically

You are now ready to assemble the correct *Asset Allocation Strategy* for your unique situation. Why you *must* do it is easy. As discussed, it is a determining factor in your portfolio's performance over 90% of the time! **Asset Allocation** is diversifying your investments in a strategic way across asset classes in order to maximize return for a given level of risk or decrease risk for a given level of return.

The generic categories consist of items previously reviewed—U.S. Stocks, U.S. Bonds, Foreign Stocks, Foreign Bonds and Cash Instruments. There are also many subsets of these general categories, such as growth stocks, high yielding stocks, small capitalization stocks, etc.

You need to match your objectives with the correct generic categories as defined by the 1 to 5 scale. To do this you need to know the approximate historical return of each category. Although this changes over time, the historical returns can generally be approximated as follows:

1 - 1.5	3% - 6% average annual return
1.5 - 2.5	6% - 10% average annual return
2.5 - 3.5	10% - 15% average annual return

Note: Keep in mind that we generally only use 1 to 3.5 for the reasons mentioned in Law 2.

These are long-term averages and are no exact indication of how any particular investment may perform. However, it is a simple chart which can be of great assistance. It matches fluctuation with possible return. At the very least it shows that one cannot achieve a 19% average annual return with an investment rated 1. In addition, keep in mind that these are *averages* and actual returns over the years will be substantially higher in some years and substantially lower (if not a loss) in other years.

Once you have decided your general range of fluctuation tolerance as an investor, the next step is to build a diversified portfolio in such a way as to achieve the return you are seeking. For example, if you have decided that you would like to achieve an approximate 12% per year average return which equates to about a 3 on our 1 to 5 scale, you need to assemble a portfolio that averages out to a 3, using the list found in Law 2. For instance, you might have certain items rated 2 (Long-term Corporate Bonds), 2.5 (Convertible Bonds), 2.75 (High Income Stocks), 3 (Growth and Value Stocks), 3.25 (Foreign Growth) and 3.5 (Small Capitalization Companies).

This is both an art and a science. There is no one correct answer. In addition, these positions can be changed as warranted (but *not* in a market timing sense) as your goals change or other factors dictate, such as resignation of the fund manager, change in the fund's objectives, etc. You should never overdo changes however, or switch funds for short-term performance reasons.

It next must be decided what percentage of your portfolio you will invest in these various asset classes. It could be an equal amount in each or you can "stack the deck" more toward one category than another. This is the *asset allocation* portion of the equation. The decision of which asset classes to use or which funds to use is the *diversification* portion of the formula. Both are needed for optimum success.

In assembling the portfolio it is not our purpose to be too technical or statistical. We could become too complex very easily as terms such as "betas" and "standard deviations" are "tools of the trade" in assembling portfolios. That is why we always recommend that you find a professional you can work with if possible. It is our purpose to give you a good working knowledge in a conceptual fashion which will assist in this process. This is *not* a mysterious process however, and can be accomplished by all.

Toward this end, below are some ideas of asset allocation models that have proven successful for others. Remember, this is an art and a science. Do not try to make it into a total science by adopting a fixed model into which all seemingly similar situations are "pigeon-holed." The only right answer is the one with which you feel comfortable. I have used mutual funds in this model.

Asset Allocation Models

Funds	Conservative	Moderate	Growth	Aggressive
Bond	25%	15%	5%	0%
Balanced (Stocks & Bonds)	15%	15%	10%	0%
Growth & Income/ Equity	15%	10%	10%	10%
Growth/ Value	25%	30%	35%	40%
Foreign Stock	10%	15%	20%	25%
Small- Cap	10%	15%	20%	25%

In the bond category there are many types. Depending on your tax bracket you could use tax-free bond funds (with "dividend rollover" programs described in Law 7) or corporate bond funds. Other growth choices can be between funds that include mid-size companies or large companies, etc.

The overall goal is to reduce risk without reducing return or increase return without increasing risk. Once an asset allocation strategy is selected, you can rebalance the strategy each year, if desired, to return it percentage-wise to the starting point. This is not a necessity, however, or even recommended in most cases. The higher returns will gravitate to the higher fluctuating funds and you may want to "ride the wave" of those investments if you feel comfortable with them. I would also not rebalance if it meant creating a taxable event in the process.

Some investors might want to invest in an asset allocation fund. This can be a *fixed* fund that automatically allocates monies among several categories and may rebalance to the original percentage yearly with no taxable event. Some of these funds are *flexible* and have a free flow of monies between asset classes as market conditions warrant.

Since there are so many types of asset allocation funds with many variables, I would recommend it for only 20% to 25% of your portfolio. It would only be a larger percentage of your portfolio if you had a small dollar amount to invest and wanted to achieve great diversification immediately. In general, however, treat asset allocation funds as you would a separate asset class.

LAW 12

Know What You Need to Know to Select a Mutual Fund

We now know that Asset Allocation Strategy is the most important determining factor in portfolio performance. Investment selection, even though second, is important enough to warrant our undivided attention.

Regarding mutual fund selection, the most important point is this: Never buy a fund because it has been rated at or near the top of its category over a specific period of time. Many times these funds make the list of poorer performers at some point in the future due to reasons that are unseen at the time. Since we are investing for a period of at least 5 years, we need a *seasoned, consistent performer* that will do well over the long term. How we decide on one and how many to use is the subject of this chapter.

As with asset allocation strategy, we recommend working with investment professionals. We feel the right professional for you can be of tremendous assistance with both Asset Allocation Policy *and* Investment Selection. We use doctors, dentists, lawyers, mortgage brokers, accountants, insurance agents, hair dressers, butchers, garage mechanics, etc. for their areas of expertise even though we might know a decent amount about the subject matter. We should absolutely do the same when it comes to investing. It should be someone we like and trust. The rest seems to take care of itself. Of course, the more knowledge we have, the better off we will be, as long as we realize that too much knowledge can be dangerous to our wealth if misdirected. In a recent Securities Industry Association study, only 9% of respondents said they know everything needed to make sound financial decisions.

The right financial professional is truly invaluable. As mentioned in Law 6, in addition to helping select the right asset allocation and diversified group of funds for you, he or she can help *keep* you in the right investments during difficult times. Therefore, choosing the right investment professional could be a net gain or loss of thousands of dollars over time. It is a decision that certainly is comparable with that of choosing an attorney or accountant.

After we have decided on an asset allocation strategy we need to fill those categories with the best funds we can. We must also realize, however, that there are thousands and thousands of funds. We are closing in on 8,000, with more opening each day. No one can research or follow anything close to this number. The good news is that you don't need to.

You should try to reduce the field of candidates to a workable number, where you and/or your advisor can get to know their attributes well enough to benefit from them. About 50 diverse funds is a workable number. If they are diverse enough you should easily be able to assemble a portfolio for virtually any amount of money.

You should compile a list long enough so that there are enough funds in each category of fund listed in Law 2. To help you produce a list (your advisor should already have one), below are some questions that need to be answered.

1. *How long has it been in existence?*
   Four to five years minimum is ideal. It can be newer only if the manager(s) has a good long-term track record elsewhere.

2. *How long has the manager been there?*
   Hopefully a great percentage of its existence.

3. *How has it performed over the long term in its specific class?*

4. *How has it done in bad markets?*
   Anyone can do well in up markets. How little it loses in rough times is most important.

You are hiring a *person* as the fund manager and for what he or she can do to benefit your life. There are many more questions we could ask to make the fund selection process more scientific, complex, or impressive. However, in the end, it boils down to people.

Doesn't it with all the professionals we rely on? You should keep the information gathering process simple and include the basics only. The information needed can be found in the prospectus, accompanying brochures, or mutual fund research and data services such as Morningstar or Lipper.

Keep in mind if using mutual fund services to use them for information only. Their own ratings may be dependent upon superfluous items and events. They, of course, would like to make you feel that fund selection is the be all and end all. It is important, but you now know the "big picture" perspective and where fund selection fits in the overall game plan. You should not worry about this aspect of investing. With these guidelines you will know a good investment selection when you see it.

It is important to remember that nothing is carved in stone. Minds can be changed. That will keep the pressure off and prevent you from doing unending and unnecessary research at the expense of higher priority tasks.

One last point on fund selection. When searching for your overall menu of possibilities, although it should include funds from each asset class, I do not recommend choosing funds that are so-called "sector" funds. These are generally funds representing various industries, such as electronics, health care, durable goods, etc. Sector funds also include single country or regional funds such as those solely representing Japan or the Far East, or Europe or Latin America.

These types of funds are too volatile. They encourage the worst of all possible strategies—trading. As soon as one sector makes the headlines and everyone jumps aboard, it is almost always time to go in the opposite direction. Leave this type of investing to others.

There is always much discussion in the press about fund "families" and why you should pick a fund family first and a particular fund second. This is in reverse order. Many times people have asked me what I think of Fidelity or Janus or Twentieth Century. When I ask them which specific fund in that company, they actually are puzzled. They do not know that they need to buy a specific fund and not a fund family. Your search for the right fund will naturally lead you to others in the same fund group. This is fine and can be looked at as a bonus. Your portfolio will be easier to administer by having two or more funds with the same management company. However, only invest in multiple funds in that family if they are the correct ones for you. Having more than one fund in the same group should not be the overriding factor in your decision making process. You are looking for the best funds for you. There is no best fund family.

The last part of this chapter has to do with the correct number of funds to get the job done in your particular case. This is a function of dollars invested along with your own comfort level. There is no one correct answer. Generally, though, the more money you have, the more asset classes *and* funds you will need. However, the number of funds will decline proportionately as the amount invested goes up.

For instance, if you are investing $50,000 you may want to have 5 positions. This does not mean that if you have $100,000 you need 10 positions. Actually 5 to 7 would be reasonable. There is nothing wrong with having one position if you are just starting to invest. In that case two positions actually could be inappropriate. Table 16 is a very approximate guide to help you select the number of positions.

Table 16 - Portfolio Structure

Amount Invested	Number of Positions
up to $5,000	1 - 2
$5,000 - $10,000	2 - 3
$10,001 - $25,000	2 - 4
$25,001 - $50,000	3 - 5
$50,001 - $75,000	4 - 6
$75,001 - $100,000	5 - 7
$100,001 - $150,000	6 - 9
$150,001 - $200,000	7 - 10
$200,001 - $500,000	8 - 12
$500,001 - $1,000,000	10 - 13
$1,000,001 +	13+

As you can see as you go up the scale, dollar-wise, the number of positions increases, but at a decreasing rate, to avoid over-diversification, especially at the higher dollar amounts. If you are just starting to invest your first dollar and are starting from close to ground zero, start with one position in the category which best describes your investment personality. Then dollar cost average each month to build wealth until your position reaches the limit as you've determined it, then switch to your second position. Always try to dollar cost average into as few positions as possible at a time, then after reaching a predetermined level switch to your next choice. Keep your wealth creating machine a simple well-oiled one!

LAW 13

When You Retire, Income Is Not All That's Needed

It used to be perceived that when you reach retirement your entire portfolio mix should change to reflect your new lifestyle change. "Income" was the operative word, which translated into all, or nearly all, fixed income items such as bonds and CDs. Today, nothing is further from the truth. Everyone is living longer (20 to even 30 years after retirement). Inflation will then need to be overcome for more years as prices will triple during that time frame. Since bonds are a hedge against deflation and stocks are a hedge against inflation, (as long as inflation is reasonable) the answer is obvious. You need to be in stocks for the rest of your life. The long-term risk is not owning them, even in retirement.

The Dow Jones average has gone up 100 times during periods of worldwide depression, two world wars, and the cold war which threatened the existence of mankind. With the downfall of Communism and the revival of Capitalism, we should be able to continue to overcome inflation and taxation over the long term.

Table 17 lends credence to this philosophy by showing what happens when income is derived from growth.

Table 17 - Living Off Capital— The Right Way!

Assume:
1. Historical average of 8% growth in share prices and a 3% dividend payout
2. You invest $100,000 in stocks at retirement
3. You need $7,000 per year to supplement income

Year	Portfolio Value	Spending During Year	Portfolio Value After Spending
1	$100,000	$7,000	$104,000
2	$104,000	$7,000	$108,440
3	$108,440	$7,000	$113,370
4	$113,370	$7,000	$118,840
5	$118,840	$7,000	$124,910

Year	Portfolio Value	Spending During Year	Portfolio Value After Spending
6	$124,910	$7,000	$131,650
7	$131,650	$7,000	$139,130
8	$139,130	$7,000	$147,440
9	$147,440	$7,000	$156,660
10	$156,660	$7,000	$166,890
11	$166,890	$7,000	$178,250
12	$178,250	$7,000	$190,850
13	$190,850	$7,000	$204,850
14	$204,850	$7,000	$220,380
15	$220,380	$7,000	$237,620
16	$237,620	$7,000	$256,630
17	$256,630	$7,000	$277,160
18	$277,160	$7,000	$299,330
19	$299,330	$7,000	$323,280
20	$323,280	$7,000	$349,140

In other words, in this example, you can withdraw 7% of your investment each year during retirement and over 20 years withdraw $140,000 and still have $349,140 in your stock account! If you invested solely in bonds at a 7% historical return, you would have only your original deposit ($100,000) at the end of 20 years. If you had used CDs at an average rate of anything less than 7% (a high probability) you would have less than your original principal and could actually run out of money well before the 20-year period. Remember, Americans' greatest fear is outliving their money. The above example assures that you won't if you make the right choices.

As stated, some people are hoping against hope that interest rates will rise again to the double digit rates seen during the 1980s, so that they can lock in high CD rates in order to accomplish their goals. This strategy is akin to "whistling in the dark." Because the 1980s are in our recent memory, we tend to think that its high interest rates might soon return. However, the 1980s from a historical viewpoint was an aberration. It would obviously be unwise to think that interest rates will return to the level of the 1980s and that a strategy could be built around buying CDs or bonds and being able to outpace inflation and taxation.

Yes, it is more difficult to put up with the periodic shocks that equity markets have during your retirement. Greed is less and fear is more. For this reason we outline below some well-known shocks and how the markets performed afterward.

Bad News and Panic Markets

1950   North Korea invaded South Korea on Sunday, June 25. The S&P 500 fell 8% to bottom at 17.44 six days later. Exactly six months later, the market made a new high of 20.43, a 17.1% increase from the bottom.

1962   The Cuban Missile Crisis occurred in October. When the U.S. set up a naval blockade of Russian ships, the market declined 6.5% in a matter of 13 days. Less than a month later, the S&P

500 had rallied to a level of 62.41, up 16.6%. A new bull market began.

1967   The Mideast War started in June. A 6.3% decline was experienced from the May 5 level of 94.44 less than a month later. A new high of 97.59 was achieved in less than seven weeks.

1987   Stock market crashed on October 19. The S&P 500 declined 20.4% in one day. By year end, 9.8% of the loss had been recovered, and the bull market continued.

1989   Mini-crash occurred on October 13. The S&P 500 experienced a 6.1% decline, which brought it to 333.65. Approximately 9 months later, the market had reached a new high of 368.95, a 10.5% gain.

At the time of their occurrence, these events spelled panic in the market. However, history tends to show a single event does not have the capacity to overwhelm the long-term growth of the free enterprise system of the U.S. economy. (See Law 3)

In retirement we need to solidify this concept in our mind. Yes, we need income from our investments in retirement. However, income should really mean getting paid back from our investments. Your asset allocation policy should be right for you and include the right percentage of growth. If invested in mutual funds, you can then use the systematic withdrawal benefit to obtain a check each month and gain the "income" you need while still having your investments increase in value.

LAW 14

During Your Working Years Use Retirement Accounts to the Fullest Extent

A common question is "How much should I put into my retirement plan at work?" Although there is no one right answer for everyone, there is a philosophy which should be adhered to: Use your retirement plan to the fullest extent possible by law or the fullest extent you can in your particular circumstances.

Why are we saying this? The answer is simple arithmetic. If you are in an approximate 30% tax bracket, and you have a retirement plan at work which allows you to invest pre-tax dollars, then you make 30%, in effect, on your money in that year. For example, if your salary is $50,000 and you deposit $6,000 in a retirement plan at work, you would report to the government that you only made $44,000. By not reporting $6,000 as income you are saving $1800 in taxes in that year ($6,000 x 30%).

It is very hard to find a competing investment that would earn 30% in any one year. In addition, all money that the $6,000 earns is tax-deferred, meaning that you do not have to pay taxes on its earnings until money is pulled out later on in life when you retire. As we have seen in Law 7, even after paying taxes, you will have much more money than if you had paid taxes each year.

On top of all this, many companies "match" your contribution up to a certain level, many times 50¢ for each dollar. Between taxes not paid, matching and tax deferral, you can easily see why retirement plans are so popular, and deservedly so. The example we just used was that of a 401(k) plan, a retirement plan named after a section of the tax code, which has been adopted by many companies. Contributions in 401(k) plans have a fixed limit, almost $10,000 per year if employee funded. There is also a similar counterpart called a 403(b) plan for non-profit organizations.

The only disadvantage of these types of plans is that they have been set up for the long-term, similar to tax deferred variable annuities. Withdrawals before age 59½ carry a 10% IRS penalty in addition to taxes on the distribution. There are provisions in many plans for hardship, but they still should be thought of as long-term vehicles. Should you leave your place of employment or be terminated, you are allowed to "roll-over" your account to your own Individual Retirement Account (IRA).

Should you be in this position, I would highly recommend rolling over the account. You will have more flexibility when you retire. Left at the original company, you will be given several choices which are fixed, unchangeable, and inflexible. For example, one possibility is a life annuity which calculates how long you will live according to actuarial tables and pays you principal and interest for life. The problem with this choice is that the calculation takes into account a fixed return, usually low, which does not give enough income to many. And since it is fixed, it will not buy as much over time. On the other hand, if the payment should be too much money per month (money you can't spend) then the excess must be again invested and the earnings achieved possibly be taxed again.

Another problem with this type of option is that if you die shortly after your payments begin, your spouse would not collect the balance unless you chose a joint and survivor annuity. However, this choice is based on two lives and therefore pays even less. Usually there are other choices, such as a lump sum distribution or a certain-period annuity. If you die, in the latter case, payments go to your spouse for a certain period, usually the balance of a 10-year period. All these choices have drawbacks, which is why we recommend rolling the account over to your own personal IRA Rollover Account for maximum flexibility regarding distribution **and** investment choices.

Today, most 401(k) plans have good "menus" of investment vehicles, allowing mutual fund investing, even though many times with only one company. When as one "slice" of your overall investment "pie." Therefore you should assemble your overall asset allocation strategy including monies in your retirement plan.

If you are not eligible or do not have a retirement plan at work, you may be eligible for an IRA and to include your spouse in a separate spousal IRA. Your eligibility depends on your income under these circumstances. You may be eligible for a full IRA (currently $2,000 per year) or a partial IRA, depending on income. The higher your income, the smaller the IRA allowed. Check with your financial advisor or accountant to calculate your eligibility. Even if you are not eligible for a tax-deductible IRA, you may still be eligible for a non-tax-deductible IRA where you can take advantage of tax-deferral. The amount in this case is limited, however, unlike your ability to use tax-deferred variable annuities (see Law 7) which are unlimited.

If your career situation is that of a self-employed individual or a small business employer, you can take advantage of several other retirement vehicles. These include SEP-IRAs or SIMPLE IRAs. A SEP-IRA stands for Simplified Employer Pension-Individual Retirement Account. You can use this vehicle whether you are self-employed (even as a sideline to your career as an employee) with no employees or in a small business with a limited number of employees.

This plan allows you to contribute for yourself but you must also contribute the same percentage for any qualified employee, which depends on age, income and time with the company. The maximum contribution currently works out to $22,500 for yourself (up to 15% of your income to a maximum income of $150,000 per year). Your business structure can be as a sole proprietor, corporation or partnership. There is no annual tax filing necessary, hence the first word in its title—*Simplified.*

Your investment choices are almost totally flexible and include all mutual funds from virtually all companies. There is usually a $10-20 per year administration charge. Funds deposited belong to each employee and he or she must manage his or her own funds. Similar to other retirement plans, withdrawals before age 59½ are subject to a 10% IRS penalty plus taxes on distributions. Be sure to check with your accountant for possible exceptions. Distributions must take place at age 70½ even if it is the minimum allowable distribution.

A SIMPLE IRA stands for Savings Incentive Match Plan for Employees. It is for businesses with 100 or fewer employees and is similar to a 401(K) but easier to administer. Companies must match contributions dollar for dollar up to 3% of pay or kick in a flat 2% for everyone. Annual employee contributions are limited to $6,000 and money taken out in the first two years is subject to a 25% early withdrawal penalty. In this vehicle participants are allowed to invest any way they choose, similar to other retirement plans previously discussed.

A SIMPLE 401(K) is an almost identical vehicle with a few exceptions. Its structure allows for loans to participants and also allows for hardship withdrawals. These plans are called SIMPLE for another reason, as there is little government reporting and fiduciary obligations.

In summary, retirement plans are a wealth creator as they contain benefits not seen elsewhere. The government and sometimes your employer will leverage this type of investment for your benefit. It is therefore obvious to go for the maximum if your financial circumstances warrant it.

LAW 15

Only Invest in Things You Completely Understand

Although this law sounds like common sense, I am amazed as to how many people do not follow it. I have come across many investors who are extremely level-headed in almost all areas of their lives, who wind up with a complicated limited partnership which is only understood by the general partner.

As a general rule of thumb, I would recommend only investing in the "mainstream" type of investments. These would include financial instruments such as stocks, bonds, mutual funds, tax-deferred annuities, retirement accounts, etc.

If you should be one of those rare individuals who have expertise in specific areas and *completely* understand all ramifications of the investment, then, of course, that would fall into the "exception" category. These investments include rental property, venture capital, limited partnerships (real estate, oil and gas, equipment leasing, etc.), hard assets, collectibles (rare coins, rare stamps, etc.) and mortgages.

In order to know whether you should invest in these areas, try explaining how they work to others. If you are confused while explaining it or sense that they are confused by listening to it, you have found your answer. We have found this to be an excellent "acid test." It is rare indeed that amateurs can pull this experiment off without a hitch.

When you start thinking about the complications of limited partnerships, about the expertise needed to succeed in the rare stamp market, or about the time needed to manage rental property, you may hopefully gravitate back to more traditional investments. Yes, there are exceptions. Some people have expertise in some of the items mentioned, a common one being equipment leasing. However, between stocks, bonds, mutual funds, tax-deferred accounts and retirement plans, there are more than enough generic choices to succeed during your lifetime. There is no need to get exotic and try to force an investment into your portfolio that has a real risk of losing a substantial portion of capital. Stick to things that fluctuate but do not carry risk of significant loss of capital over the long-term.

LAW 16

Never, Ever Buy an Investment over the Phone

Although this law sounds like even more common sense than Law 15, it is constantly being violated. I cannot figure out why people do this, but they do, every day. Would you take advice from (and pay the fee to) an attorney or accountant who cold-called you on the phone? Would you take out a mortgage from a mortgage broker who solicited you on the phone? Would you buy a house through an unseen real estate broker? The same thing goes for investments. I believe that greed has a lot to do with people buying investments over the phone.

If you combine not buying investments that you don't completely understand (Law 15) with not buying investments over the phone, you will be well on your way to avoiding investment catastrophes.

LAW 17

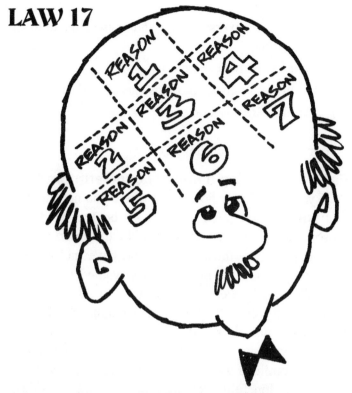

Keep the 7 Reasons People Fail to Accumulate Wealth in the Front of Your Mind

Below are listed the seven (7) reasons people fail to accumulate as much wealth as they could or should. After interviewing hundreds of investors and reviewing their portfolios, I can say that the list is almost as valid today (and probably will be tomorrow) as it was when originally drawn up. The seven reasons are as follows:

1. Failure to develop a sound long-term strategy
2. Bearing too much or too little risk

3. Poor advisors
4. Inadequate diversification and/or inadequate asset allocation
5. Poor investment selection
6. Failure to control emotions (greed and fear)
7. Paying excessive taxes

Let us look at each item:

Failure to Develop a Sound Long-Term Strategy

If you don't know how to get where you need to get, you will not get there. This is #1 on the list for a reason. It is the most important. In the interviews I have conducted, those people who have had a clear and even written list of goals they wanted to accomplish financially were over halfway to success. The strategy will follow (hopefully after reading this book!) If a goal is not clear and written it is merely a wish, which may or may not come true. If the strategy is not precisely outlined with great vision, the result will not be visible. Hopefully, you are now prepared to do this.

Bearing Too Much or Too Little Risk

This is the reason we devised our 1 to 5 scale. It is to enable someone to see risk more clearly. As mentioned, we prefer to use the word **fluctuation** instead of risk, as it more accurately describes the action of mainstream investments (stocks, bonds, etc.) over the long term. By having a scale that is able to compare investments *to each other* we can get a feel for what its fluctuation may approximate. It is not a fixed reading compared to the market average (called a "beta"), but a guide to assist an investor *comparing* various types of investments while assembling his or her portfolio.

Poor Advisors

Whom you choose to work with will be a major factor in your success. Make sure you are periodically reviewing your advisor to make sure you are on the same "wave length" in accomplishing your goals.

Inadequate Diversification and Asset Allocation

This is self-explanatory. It is the reason for Laws #8 and #11. Taken together, they are the essence of assembling the best possible portfolio for the long haul.

Poor Investment Selection

Although we now know that asset allocation policy is much more the determining factor in performance, investment selection is still important. The best strategy is to assemble your smaller "menu" of investments to a workable number.

Failure to Control Emotions (Greed and Fear)

These are the two emotions which guide money and investments our whole lives. I found that once fear is overcome, greed can follow. As stated, the important thing is to keep an even keel between these two. A certain amount of fear is healthy, as is a certain amount of greed. Hopefully the concepts presented in this book will help you to keep your balance. That is, they will reduce fear to a point that will enable you to move ahead, and keep greed in check so as not to do anything foolish.

Paying Excessive Taxes

This is another important item (see Law 7). If a person is in the 33% tax bracket and he has eliminated or deferred taxes on unearned income on his tax return, he has achieved a 33% better return before anything else happens. This can occur by contributing to a retirement plan, tax-free account or tax-deferred account. By contributing to a retirement plan, taxes on earned income are also reduced, creating an even greater overall return.

Summary

If I had to describe a successful investment portfolio I would do so as follows:

A successful investment portfolio is one where the return meets your future needs after inflation and taxation combined. An unsuccessful investment portfolio is one where the return does not even exceed inflation and taxation combined.

I sincerely wish you the best of luck in making your money work as hard for you as you did for it!

Questions and Answers

Below are some commonly asked questions I have encountered and their answers. Although the answers can be found in the text for the most part, this format can help in the learning process. They are in no particular order:

1. *"Will there be another stock market crash?"*

Yes. History has shown that. After every bull market comes a bear market and vice-versa. Some bear markets are very short and are called crashes. It must not deter you, however, in your long-term strategy. Crashes and bear markets are a necessity that enable markets to cleanse themselves (dry up speculation) and eventually move forward. It also gives astute investors an opportunity to participate in the markets at reduced prices. If there were a sale on suits or other items you would circle the day on your calendar so as not to miss it. Sales in investments are much more profitable!

2. *"I would like to take no risk in my investments. Can I do that and get a good return?"*

No. What you have described is a savings vehicle, one with no fluctuation. As long as you are investing for the long term, we can call it fluctuation, and not risk. The biggest risk of all in the long run is the risk of loss of purchasing power. This occurs when your investments do not do well enough for you to meet your future needs.

3. *"Should I try to find a professional to help me?"*

Yes. There are certain issues that must be addressed in order to obtain the results you want. These issues include: How are you going to allocate and diversify your portfolio for maximum gain? What will you do when markets inevitably go against you? Do you have the training and temperament to act without panic? As your life changes and your goals change, do you have the ability to adapt accordingly? Do you have the time to do all these things? Sometimes we are not the best people to judge our course of action in these situations and we need assistance.

Morningstar Financial Services recently completed a study of the performance of 219 growth mutual funds over a 5-year period ending in 1994. They found that these funds averaged 12.5% annual return. However, when they analyzed what each individual investor made, they found an astonishing average **loss** of 2.2%! How could this be? It comes from investors without advisors who panicked at various junctures in the 5-year cycle and only held those funds for an average of 17 months. It pays to have an experienced professional at your side for this reason alone.

4. *"So and so (in the media) just reported on an economy in trouble. Does this affect our strategy?"*

No. If we listened to the media we would never be able to send our children to college or retire. Ignore it. Negativism sells and they must fill air time. Where is the story in the media about how well this country has done economically this century?

5. *"What should be my overall goal?"*

In an overall sense, you should look to *create and manage wealth*. There are 3 ways to do this:

1. Increase Returns
2. Decrease Taxes
3. Have a Disciplined System to Invest From Income

If done properly this will put you in a position to live off your wealth no matter how long you live or no matter what the rate of inflation becomes.

As you can see, this is quite a short list. Most questions are usually repetitious, general in nature and fall under the categories represented above. When answering people's questions, I try to include the appropriate concepts from the list of basics below:

- Investments go up and down (a tough one for people to believe!)
- Most people, without professional guidance, do the wrong thing at the wrong time (even when right, they are prone to change their minds.)
- Markets overreact (they do *not* do what experts say they will do.)
- No one knows what the future will bring.
- Diversification and Asset Allocation carry the day.
- Savings accounts and CDs will not make you rich.
- Uncertainty creates opportunity.
- Never say never (e.g.: "Interest rates will never go below 6%," etc.).

Handy Tools

This section includes some handy tools to assist you. I have used all of these in helping clients at one time or another. Hopefully some will apply to you at some point.

Risk/Reward of Interest Rates - Treasury Bonds

Impact of Interest Rate Rises on Value of Bonds				
Rise	5-Year	10-Year	20-Year	30-Year
.5%	–2.2%	–3.7%	–5.3%	–6.1%
1.0%	–4.3%	–7.1%	–10.2%	–11.6%
1.5%	–6.3%	–10.4%	–14.7%	–16.6%
2.0%	–8.3%	–13.7%	–18.1%	–21.1%

Impact of Interest Rate Declines on Value of Bonds				
Decline	5-Year	10-Year	20-Year	30-Year
.5%	2.2%	+3.8%	+5.7%	+6.7%
1.0%	+4.5%	+7.8%	+11.8%	+14.2%
1.5%	+6.8%	+12.0%	+18.6%	+22.5%
2.0%	+9.2%	+14.4%	+25.9%	+31.8%

Note: After seeing this chart investors usually want to put more, percentage-wise, into equities as the swings in bonds are generally more than perceived.

Should You Cash in Your CD?

What annualized rate you must have in a new investment to justify paying the early withdrawal penalty of your current CD. Check your particular bank to get the exact amount. The returns below represent the average bank.

Time Remaining on Current CD, Months							
Current CD Rate	6	12	18	24	36	48	60
3.0%	4.51%	3.75%	3.50%	3.38%	3.25%	3.19%	3.15%
3.5%	5.26%	4.38%	4.09%	3.94%	3.79%	3.72%	3.68%
4.0%	6.02%	5.01%	4.67%	4.50%	4.34%	4.25%	4.20%
4.5%	6.77%	5.64%	5.26%	5.07%	4.88%	4.78%	4.73%
5.0%	7.53%	6.26%	5.84%	5.63%	5.42%	5.32%	5.25%
5.5%	8.28%	6.89%	6.43%	6.20%	5.96%	5.85%	5.78%
6.0%	9.04%	7.52%	7.01%	6.76%	6.51%	6.38%	6.30%
6.5%	9.80%	8.15%	7.60%	7.32%	7.05%	6.91%	6.83%
7.0%	10.56	8.78%	8.18%	7.89%	7.59%	7.44%	7.36%
7.5%	11.32	9.41%	8.77%	8.45%	8.14%	7.98%	7.88%
8.0%	12.07	10.04	9.36%	9.02%	8.68%	8.51%	8.41%

Converting Total Returns

	Cumulative	
Annualized	**3 Years**	**5 Years**
5%	15.8%	27.6%
6%	19.1%	33.8%
7%	22.5%	40.3%
8%	26.0%	46.9%
9%	29.5%	53.9%
10%	33.1%	61.1%
11%	36.8%	68.5%
12%	40.5%	76.2%
13%	44.3%	84.2%
14%	48.2%	92.5%
15%	52.1%	101.1%
16%	56.1%	110.0%
17%	60.2%	119.2%
18%	64.3%	128.8%
19%	68.5%	138.6%
20%	72.8%	148.8%

Retirement Cash Needs

Pre-retirement Income	% Needed in Retirement	% Replaced by Social Security	% You Need from Pensions & Savings
$20,000	76%	64%	12%
$30,000	72	55	17
$40,000	71	44	27
$50,000	74	37	37
$60,000	74	31	43
$70,000	77	27	50
$80,000	84	23	61
$90,000	86	21	65
$150,000	86	13	73
$200,000	87	9	78
$250,000	89	8	81

Important Note: These percentages are a guide only. Each person's lifestyle goals are different. In addition, these percentages do *not* take into account inflation or taxation.

Retirement Plan Descriptions

Type of Plan	SEP (Simplified Employer Pension) also known as SEP-IRA
Brief Description	Employer-funded retirement plan in which employer establishes IRAs for eligible employees and self
Targeted Business Organization	Sole proprietorships, corporations, partnerships, state and local governments, unincorporated businesses and tax exempt organizations
Benefits to Employer	• Retirement savings for self and employees • No annual tax filing necessary
Source of Contributed Funds	• Employer funded • Owner makes contribution for self and employees • Employer must contribute same percentage for all
Maximum Contributions	Owner may contribute lesser of 15% of each eligible employee's earned income up to $22,500
Employee Limitations	None. An unlimited number of eligible employees may participate
Employee Eligibility Requirements	• Age 21 • Compensation from employer $374 or more (1992 index) • Employed by owner for 3 of preceding 5 years
Deadlines: Opening/Funding	• April 15 or the business' tax filing deadline (plus extensions)
Investment Choices	• FDIC CDs and IMMAs • Self-Directed Brokerage IRA products • Portfolio IRA (Mutual Funds)
Investment Decisions	Deposited funds belong to employee and he/she must manage the funds
Withdrawing Funds	• Distributions prior to age 59½ may be subject to 10% IRS penalty • Distributions subject to income tax
Special Points	Owner cannot make a contribution to his/her own SEP account without making a contribution to the account of eligible employees

Type of Plan	401(k)
Brief Description	A profit-sharing retirement plan that permits employee and employer contributions
Targeted Business Organization	Corporations and self-employed business owners
Benefits to Employer	• Flexibility in providing a cherished employee benefit
Source of Contributed Funds	• Elective employee salary deferrals • Matching employer contributions • Non-elective employer contributions • After-tax voluntary contributions
Maximum Contributions	• If funded by employee: the lesser of 15% of earned income or $9,240 (1995) • If funded by employer or combination employee/employer: the lesser of 15% of earned income or $22,500
Employee Limitations	None. All eligible employees may participate.
Employee Eligibility Requirements	• One year of service • Minimum age must not be above 21
Deadlines: Opening/Funding	• Last day of business' tax year, usually December 31 • April 15 or the business' tax filing deadline (plus extensions)
Investment Choices	• Mutual funds or annuities made available by plan administrator
Investment Decisions	Employee makes own choices within plan options
Withdrawing Funds	• Hardship withdrawals permitted • Distributions prior to age 59½ may be subject to 10% IRS penalty • Distributions subject to income tax
Special Points	• Matching contributions are an added employee incentive

Type of Plan	403(b) (TSA - Tax Sheltered Annuity)
Brief Description	A tax-sheltered annuity retirement program for employees of specific types of businesses or non-profit organizations
Targeted Business Organization	Tax-exempt charitable, educational or religious organizations, health care institutions
Benefits to Employer	● No obligation to fund
Source of Contributed Funds	● Elective employee salary deferrals
Maximum Contributions	Generally the lesser of $9,500 or 20% of earned income
Employee Limitations	None.
Employee Eligibility Requirements	None.
Deadlines: Opening/Funding	None.
Investment Choices	Fixed and variable annuities
Investment Decisions	Employee chooses from among several annuity companies the type of annuity desired
Withdrawing Funds	● Withdrawals prior to 59½ may be subject to insurance company surrender fees as well as IRS penalties ● Distributions subject to income tax
Special Points	● Exclusively funded through employee contributions ● Invested primarily in insurance contracts

Type of Plan	SIMPLE IRA (Savings Incentive Match Plan for Employees)
Funding	Employee salary deferral contributions Mandatory employer contributions (matching or non elective).
Participation Requirements	Businesses with 100 or fewer eligible employees who do not maintain another retirement plan.
Contributions	Employee: May not exceed the lesser of $6,000 or 100% of employee annual taxable compensation. Employer: Dollar-for-dollar match up to 3% of compensation for all eligible employees. (Special rule: can lower percentage, but not below 1%, for any two out of every five years.) OR 2% non-elective contributions for all eligible employees.
Annual Administration	No testing required.
Taxation	Employee contributions are made on a pre-tax basis, excludable from income. Employer matching contributions are deductible (if made by due date, including extensions, for employer's tax return).
Eligibility	Employees that earn at least $5,000 in compensation during the prior two years and who are reasonably expected to receive $5,000 during the coming year.
Loans	Not permitted.
Withdrawals	There is a two-year waiting period before money can be rolled over into an IRA. However, assets can be rolled from one SIMPLE account to another SIMPLE account. Withdrawals are subject to a 25% tax penalty during the first two years if under age 59½; 10% penalty after two years if under age 59½.
Distribution	Distributions are generally taxed under rules governing IRAs.
Participant Vesting	Immediate 100% vesting.

To reach the author

Richard Rodman, President
Tax Relief Investments, Inc.
215 North Avenue West, Suite 360
Westfield, NJ 07090
(908) 654-8041
(908) 654-6707 fax

Securities affiliation with
Investment Advisors and Consultants, Inc.
Ocean, NJ

Index

Give the Gift of
Successful Investing to
Your Friends and Colleagues
Check Your Leading Bookstore or Order Here

☐ **YES**, I want ___ copies of *The 17 Laws of Successful Investing* at $14.95 each, plus $3 shipping per book (New Jersey residents please add 90¢ state sales tax per book). Canadian orders must be accompanied by a postal money order in U.S. funds. Allow 15 days for delivery.

☐ **YES**, I am interested in having Richard Rodman speak or give a seminar to my company, association, school, or organization. Please send information.

My check or money order for $_____ is enclosed.
Please charge my ☐ Visa ☐ MasterCard

Name_____
Phone _____
Organization _____
Address _____
City/State/Zip _____
Card # _____ Exp. Date _____
Signature _____

Please make your check payable and return to:
Alidan Press
215 North Avenue West, Suite 360
Westfield, NJ 07090

Call your credit card order to:
1-800-507-BOOK
Fax: 908-654-6707